Just a Minute!

Maple Tree Press books are published by Owlkids Books Inc.
10 Lower Spadina Avenue, Suite 400, Toronto, Ontario M5V 2Z2
www.owlkids.com

Distributed in Canada by Raincoast Books
9050 Shaughnessy Street, Vancouver, British Columbia V6P 6E5

Distributed in the United States by Publishers Group West
1700 Fourth Street, Berkeley, California 94710

Dedication
For Danielle, who I enjoy spending many minutes with

Cataloguing in Publication Data
Szpirglas, Jeff
    Just a minute! : a crazy adventure in time / by Jeff Szpirglas ;
illustrated by Stephen MacEachern.

ISBN 978-1-897349-44-1 (bound).   ISBN 978-1-897349-45-8 (pbk.)

    1. Time—Juvenile fiction. 2. Time—Juvenile literature.
I. MacEachern, Stephen II. Title.

QB209.5.S96 2009   jC813'.6   C2008-907618-4

Library of Congress Control Number: 2008941717

Design & illustrations: Stephen MacEachern

We acknowledge the financial support of the Canada Council for the
Arts, the Ontario Arts Council, the Government of Canada through
the Book Publishing Industry Development Program (BPIDP), and
the Government of Ontario through the Ontario Media Development
Corporation's Book Initiative for our publishing activities.

Printed in China

A   B   C   D   E   F

Just a Minute!

A Crazy Adventure in Time

Jeff Szpirglas

Illustrated by
Stephen MacEachern

MAPLE
TREE
PRESS

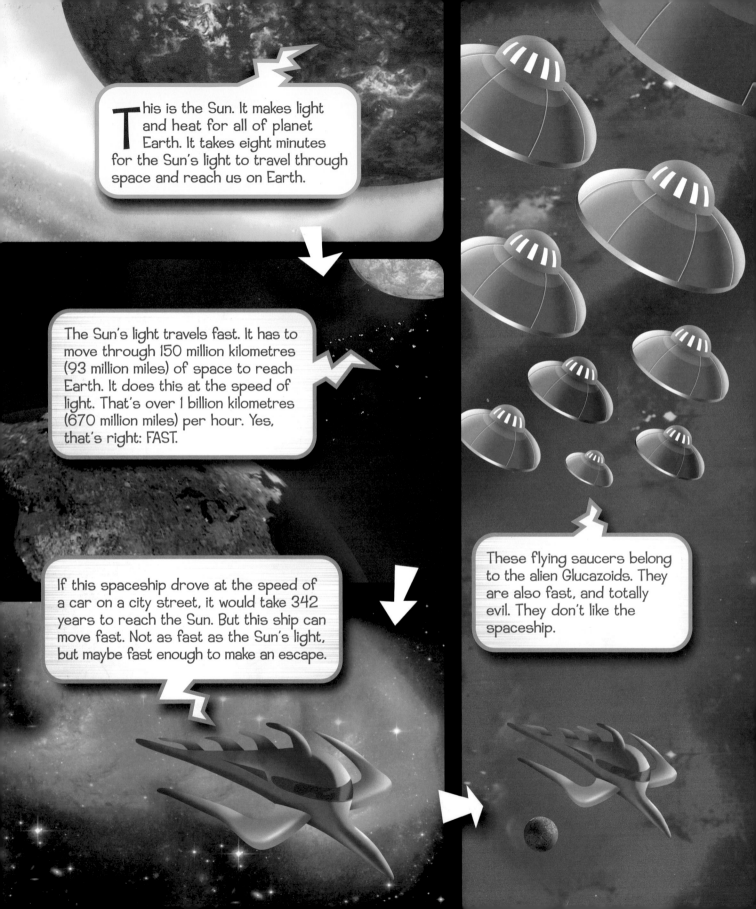

Pandas eat bamboo. The world's fastest-growing bamboo can grow almost 1 millimetre (less than four-hundredths of an inch) in one minute. It may not seem like much, but this bamboo could grow 1 metre (3 feet) in a single day!

It takes around a minute for a toilet to flush and refill. It uses around 6 litres (1 $\frac{1}{2}$ gallons) of water for each flush. That's enough to fill three large soda bottles. (By the way, don't fill soda bottles from the toilet, please!)

A big-city newspaper prints over 600 copies, or around 50,000 pages, each minute.

This man reading a newspaper page is moving his eyes back and forth around 240 times a minute to read 300 words.

If 50,000 newspaper pages were spread out and laid end to end, they'd stretch out 28 kilometres (17 miles). That's farther than a half-marathon race course!

HOLLYWOOD MOVIE SHOOT COMES TO TOWN

Meanwhile, inside the plant pavilion, things are flapping...

In just one second, a spider can drop down 30 centimetres (12 inches) on a string of silk.

A swallowtail butterfly beats its wings around 300 times a minute.

It takes an orb weaver spider forty-five to sixty minutes (about an hour) to spin a web.

A housefly beats its wings around 9,000 times a minute.

It takes a Venus flytrap one-tenth of a second to catch a fly. It spends about seven days eating it, though! That's 10,080 minutes of digestion.

6

Venus Flytrap

When a camel is really, really thirsty, it can drink about 8 litres (2 gallons) of water in a minute—about half of a water cooler jug.

A camel can keep drinking until it's full—at around 80 litres (20 gallons). That's over twenty times the amount of water an adult human stomach can hold!

Speaking of lots of water, enough water rushes over Niagara Falls in one minute to fill nearly 140 Olympic-sized pools! That's enough water to quench the thirst of 2.25 million parched camels each minute!

An anaconda could spend up to forty minutes underwater at one time!

Here's a fact without any cows: traction elevators (pulled from the top with steel rope) in high-rise buildings travel at about 122 metres (400 feet) per minute. That's about the height of 22 giraffes (not cows)!

Why are we so concerned about cows when there are animals escaping from the zoo? And what will happen when the animals reach the set of the BIG EXPENSIVE MOVIE that's being filmed in the city? How many minutes can you wait until you turn the page to find out?

How do you count one minute? Do you use a wristwatch? A cell phone? Maybe even the big wall clock in your classroom? Here are some other clocks people have used through history. Which do you think could count in minutes?

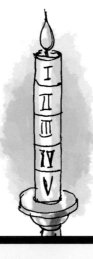

1500 BCE

Ancient Egyptians were the first people to make a clock that could be used both day and night (it wasn't reliant on shadows cast by the Sun). They marked the water level inside a big stone sink. People could then measure how much time passed by the amount of water that dripped out of a small hole in the bottom.

850 CE

The candle wasn't just used to light up dark places before electricity was discovered. It's said that the English king Alfred the Great came up with a way to tell time using a candle with markings on the side. As the wick burned down, a person could tell how many hours had passed from one mark to the next. And because it was a candle, this clock doubled as a nightlight, too!

1000 CE

Hourglass time-keepers aren't just used for board games. In medieval Europe, these glasses with squeezed-in middles poured out equal amounts of crushed eggshell to measure time. The timepiece would be turned over when the eggshells (and time) had run through.

1577

A clockmaker named Jost Burgi is credited with making the world's first minute hand on a clock to be used by astronomers (scientists who study stars).

1656

A Dutch scientist named Christiaan Huygens created the pendulum clock, that big swinging thing seen in all grandfather clocks. A pendulum swings at a steady rate, which means it can be used to keep time. This clock was a big improvement over other clocks, only going off by as little as ten seconds for every day.

1929

The next step in timekeeping used tiny crystals of quartz that were charged with electricity to power a motor and keep time. Crystal could also be used to make digital screens that used numbers instead of hands for minutes and hours.

1949

Scientists found that even tiny bits of "stuff," called atoms, could be used to keep time. They made the atomic clock. Atoms vibrate or move at the same speed, and these movements have helped to keep time to around 30 billionths of a second for every year.

Today

What's the next great invention? Time will tell!

ACKNOWLEDGMENTS

Many of the facts in this book came from studies, journals, the Internet, books, and other sources. I took the numbers and broke them down into units of time. It really helps when I can turn to people with expert knowledge of the subject matter (anything from giant anteaters to solar astronomy to cow burps). Here's a very big thank you to the people who made sure my research was accurate:

Tavis J. Basford, M.D.; Todd A. Blackledge, Ph.D., University of Akron; Richard J. Blakeslee, Ph.D., NASA Marshall Space Flight Center; Richard A. Bowen, Ph.D., Colorado State University; Kevin Richard Butt, Ph.D., University of Central Lancashire; John Byers, Ph.D., author, *Built for Speed;* Julie Cassidy; Lynn Clark, Ph.D., Iowa State University; Robert K. Colwell, Ph.D., University of Connecticut, Storrs; Richard N. Conner, Ph.D., Scientist Emeritus, Southern Research Station; Terence J. Dawson, Ph.D., University of New South Wales; Rebecca Fisher, Ph.D., Arizona State University, University of Arizona, College of Medicine-Phoenix; Dr. T. K. Gahlot, camel vet and editor, *Journal of Camel Practice and Research*; John R. Grider, Ph.D., VCU School of Medicine; Kyle Herring, NASA Public Affairs—Space Shuttle Program; Rodger Kram, Ph.D., University of Colorado; Anjali Kumar; Gordon E. Legge, Ph.D., University of Minnesota; Jackie Long, production division, *Toronto Star* newspaper; L. Timothy Long, Ph.D., School of Earth and Atmospheric Sciences, Georgia Institute of Technology; David Loewith; Timothy S. McCay, Ph.D., Colgate University; Brad Moon, Ph.D., University of Louisiana at Lafayette; Jim Nation, Ph.D., Professor Emeritus, University of Florida; Eric R. Pianka, Ph.D., University of Texas at Austin; Martin Pietrucha, Ph.D., Penn State University; Linda Rayor, Ph.D., Cornell University; Stephen Roque; R.A. Rubin, Ph.D., North Carolina State University; Stephen Secor, Ph.D., University of Alabama; James H. Shaw, Ph.D., Oklahoma State University; Evgenya Shkolnik, Ph.D., Department of Terrestrial Magnetism, Carnegie Institute of Washington; Keith Tinkler, Brock University; Transportation Division, Environment Canada; Patricia Tricorache, Cheetah Conservation Fund, http://www.cheetah.org/; Patricia A. Tun, Ph.D., Brandeis University; Johan van Leeuwen, Ph.D., Wageningen University; Iwan Williams, Ph.D., Queen Mary University of London; Karin M. Wittenberg, Ph.D., University of Manitoba; Tim R. Young, Ph.D., University of North Dakota; George Zug, author, *Snakes: Smithsonian Answer Book*. Thanks also to *Pasture Production*, Publication 19, Ministry of Agriculture, Food and Rural Affairs—for cattle grazing facts!